101
Etsy
Tips

For a Successful Shop

J. A. Case

Dedicated to my father Harley Allen Case, Jr.

The term "Etsy" is a registered trademark of Etsy, Inc.

This publication has not been licensed or approved by Etsy, Inc.

First Edition

Printed in the United States of America

10 9 8 7 6 5

CONTENTS

Introduction

Chapter 1 – First Steps

Chapter 2 – Finances

Chapter 3 – Products

Chapter 4 – Marketing

Chapter 5 – Website

Chapter 9 – Running Your Business

Chapter 6 – Get Help

Chapter 7 – Shipping

Chapter 8 – Etsy-specifics

Introduction

My Etsy journey started at a Crate & Barrel store several years ago. My wife and I were browsing the store on a lazy Sunday afternoon when we saw a wooden wall sculpture. I looked at the price tag: $600! I told my wife, "I can make that."

At that time, I was looking for a full-time job. My wife and I had recently moved to Phoenix from Houston. I was spending most of my time applying and interviewing, and since I had some free time on my hands, I decided to try making a wall sculpture similar to the one I saw at Crate & Barrel.

I didn't have any real tools at the time, nor did I have woodworking experience. I just knew that I enjoyed making things and working with my hands. I went to Home Depot, bought some wood, rebar, and heavy-duty adhesive and made a wall sculpture. It didn't turn out quite as I'd imagined, but it was okay.

After posting a photo to Instagram and getting some likes, I realized that maybe, just maybe, I could make something similar to this piece and sell it online. That idea got my wheels turning. I started designing and making prototypes. I researched better materials, I bought some tools, and then I opened my own Etsy shop.

For the first year that I had my shop, I only had eight listings, and my sales were just over $2,000. That's okay for a part-time business, as I was only dipping my toe in the water and learning along the way. I enjoyed making one or two pieces per month. For me, it was more about the satisfaction of making something for somebody, not making money.

At this point, I had no idea that my Etsy shop was about to become my full-time business. After I designed and constructed a table and put it on Etsy, things started to change. My shop started to attract more visitors, generate more likes, and engage more followers. Sales started to increase. As a result, I started thinking even bigger and did more research into other Etsy shops.

Suddenly, I went from two orders the previous month to 40 orders and $9,000 in revenue. It was exciting! Even as I sit here writing this book, I'm continuing to get orders on Etsy, and it's still exciting. It is absolutely possible to make $100,000 or more in revenue on Etsy. In fact, my best year was just under $200,000 in revenue. There are some Etsy shops making a lot more than that, too. Of course, revenue and profit are two separate things.

I cannot guarantee you that you will earn $100,000 or more per year, but if you implement these tips, you will have a better chance at succeeding on Etsy. How much you earn is largely determined by your work ethic. Put in the work, and you will see results.

There are at least four things that you will have little to no control over: timing, demand, competition, and luck. With any luck, however, the timing of your shop will be right, demand will be high, and the competition will be minimal or nonexistent. If you follow these tips and are lucky enough to have great timing, high demand, and/or little competition, you should succeed.

I have learned a lot that I wish I had known before I opened my shop. I didn't plan for success on Etsy, but you can. Before you even open your shop, you can set yourself up for success. Even if you don't decide to open an Etsy shop, most of these tips can help you operate any small business.

Chapter 1 - First Steps

RESEARCH

Do your research. Before you open your shop, study and examine the competition that already exists and take notes. It's smart to study non-competitors, too. What do you like about the shop that they seem to be doing right? What do you dislike? What catches your eye? What do customers seem to like the best? What could they be doing to improve their shop? How do they write their product descriptions? By asking all of these kinds of questions, you can gain a more honed-in idea of what you want your own shop to eventually look like.

Research is the best strategy that you can use, and it's free. It only costs your time, and it will certainly be time well-spent. If you are serious about operating a successful business, diving in and studying the competition is a great way to learn.

Choose five successful shops that you consider to be your competition, and then pick five successful shops that are not competitors. All of these shops should have high sales totals and high review ratings. You don't want to waste your time studying a brand new shop that has only 25 sales and four reviews. Sure, it might be a good shop, but you'll want to study the ones that have been around for some time.

Spend at least one hour studying each shop in detail:

- How do they write their product descriptions?
- How many listings do they have?
- How many product categories do they have?
- Do they do custom work?
- Do they ship overseas?

- What is their return policy?
- Do they offer free shipping?
- Do their photographs look professional?
- What tag words do they use?

THE RIGHT IDEA

Your first great idea will probably not be your best idea. You may have what you consider to be a great idea for a shop or a product, but there's always a chance that your next idea or your tenth idea will be the winner. It's easy to come up with one idea and then stop brainstorming. You can become obsessed with that one idea. You can focus on and spend all of your time thinking about it, how wonderful it is, how much money you will make, etc. But is it the right idea?

When you come up with an idea, you should ask yourself some basic questions: Are other people doing the same exact thing? Does your idea have a unique twist or design? What will people be willing to pay for it? Can you make a profit? Is it trendy or could it be a potential long-term business? Can you expand on and grow the idea?

My first Etsy products were wood wall sculptures inspired by mid-century design. I sold a steady one or two per month. It wasn't a huge success, but it was my first idea. That idea evolved into designing tables, which then led to a successful Etsy shop. If I hadn't started with wall sculptures, I never would have had a successful Etsy shop making tables. Even if your first idea isn't great, you can still pivot and turn your shop into a success.

MAKING THE RIGHT PRODUCT

You can sell almost anything on Etsy. You don't even have to be a maker. But, if you are a maker, then you probably have a good idea of what you plan to sell. Whether your product is made from raw, repurposed, or recycled materials, you are going to spend time and money to produce it. That time and money spent is your cost.

Your cost will determine your price which will determine your profit. If it costs you $10 in raw materials to produce a yoga mat, and it takes you one hour to create, your cost is $10 plus whatever you value your time at. If your time is valued at $15 per hour, one mat will cost you $25 to make. To make a decent profit, you probably then want to price the yoga mat at around $40, for example.

Check out the competition before setting your price. What are similar items selling for on Etsy? Can you sell your product for a higher price because it features a special material or design? Is it better than existing products being sold? Will people pay a premium for your product? These are questions to consider when deciding what you are going to make.

PARTNERSHIP AGREEMENT

Before you agree to start a business with someone, discuss it in detail and plan ahead. Have a written partnership agreement. This is to protect you, your investment, your business, your assets, and your future. Partnerships can sometimes turn sour, and there may be disagreements. You need to protect yourself from any inevitabilities.

A partnership agreement is a written contract that establishes each person's responsibilities as well as defines the profit and loss distribution of each partner. It should also cover issues regarding any rules, withdrawals, management structure, and possible dissolution. In general, this agreement should cover everything so that both parties are legally protected from any future disagreements. It's also recommended to have a business attorney review the agreement.

Even though you may not want to think about it, companies can dissolve. A partner could change their mind and may want to withdraw from a business. Various personal situations can alter someone's plans. Stuff happens. A partnership agreement exists as a roadmap for the things that you probably don't want to think about but should.

BUSINESS PLAN

Many people hear "business plan" and immediately begin to panic. Don't panic! Think of a business plan as a recipe -- you cannot make an amazing lemon meringue pie without a detailed recipe. You can try, but it probably won't turn out very well.

Writing a business plan can set you up for success. If you want your business to start off on the right foot, it's wise to take the time to write a plan. The U.S. Small Business Administration (SBA) offers business plan examples and templates, as well as many other valuable resources. Visit their website (sba.gov), and spend time reading and researching what they offer.

You don't have to write a 30-page business plan. You can begin by writing what is called a Lean Startup Plan (aka Business Model Canvas). The lean plan focuses on nine components of your business. It will help you visualize your product or service and operations strategies, identify your target customers, establish a marketing plan, and analyze your competition. If you need assistance, the SBA has counselors and mentors in every state. Take advantage of their services. It's free!

BUSINESS CHECKING ACCOUNT

Before you make your first sale, open a business checking account. You will want to keep your business expenses separate from your personal, or else it will become very confusing down the road. Opening a business checking account will solve this issue. Every bank offers business checking, but they are not all the same. Do some online research before opening an account, or make an in-person appointment at your preferred bank.

Chase Bank is rated highly and has a very large network. They also offer a cash bonus to first-time account holders. There will be some small fees, but if you maintain a minimum balance, you can avoid the monthly fee. Chase also has a mobile app where you can deposit checks, pay bills, and transfer money.

US Bank offers a business checking account with no monthly fees. They also do not charge for out-of-network ATM transactions. Like Chase, they have a mobile app where you can deposit checks. The free account has limited monthly transactions, so make sure that you read the details first.

Whichever bank you choose, start your business checking account with at least $500. Keep your business spending separate from your personal so that come tax time, you will be happy that you did.

SECRET RECIPE

I wish that I could tell you that there's a secret recipe to succeed on Etsy. It requires some special combination of design, product, number of listings, categories, tag words, and great photos. While this perfect mix doesn't exist, if you take your research seriously and do your best to learn from it, you can certainly make your own winning recipe.

Don't skip over the research. The research you do will help shape your own shop when you're ready to build it. I recommend researching at least five shops that appeal to you and that appear to be successful.

Make your own perfect recipe. If you do the research and combine that with your own ideas, designs, projections, and your unique skills, you can make an Etsy recipe that works great for you. By borrowing inspiration from existing shops and mixing in your own ideas and style, your Etsy shop can be a winner that in turn, others will want to learn from and study.

DO ONE THING AT A TIME

Don't try to do everything at once. Focus on one thing, and work on it until it's completed. When starting a new Etsy shop, it's easy to get overwhelmed with everything that you need to do. Below is a to-do list for starting your Etsy business that you can check off as you complete each task. It's important to note that you don't start working on your Etsy shop until #9.

1. Do your research
2. Brainstorm ideas
3. Have funding in place
4. Write a business plan

5. Create or acquire products
6. Photograph your products
7. Create social media accounts
8. Create a website
9. Start building your Etsy shop
10. Write your About, Story, and Policies
11. Upload your image and banner image
12. Create the listings
13. Link your website and social media to your Etsy shop
14. Open your Etsy shop
15. Start promoting! Drive traffic to your Etsy shop

Chapter 2 – Finances

FUNDING

Do you have any money saved to start your business? The beauty of Etsy is that you can start a shop with little to no money. I started my shop with no money, but I wouldn't recommend doing this. If you can save up $500 or $1,000 to launch your business, it puts you in a better and more comfortable starting point.

For the first year of my Etsy business, I was part-time. Then, nearly overnight, I went from part-time to full-time due to the amount of orders that I received in just one month. I had to fulfill all of those orders immediately, and I didn't have any extra cash set aside. Fortunately, Etsy deposits your earnings into your bank account weekly. If you received ten orders last week, that money will accrue and will be deposited into your bank account this week.

My first big month on Etsy was 40 orders which totaled $9,000. That's great, right? Well, yes and no. Since I didn't have any savings, I had to spend the incoming money to convert my part-time business into my full-time business. That $9,000 left my account as fast as it came in because I needed a lot of raw materials, tools, money for packaging, shipping, etc. I just simply didn't plan for the quick growth. Any cash you can set aside for business in the beginning is going to help when your business ramps up.

FUNDING IDEAS

There are many ways to fund your Etsy business without going into debt. Let's say that you want to start your business with $1,000 in cash.

How will you get $1,000 without using a credit card or taking out a small loan? Here's where you can be creative.

First, look around your home. Are there items that are in perfect condition that you no longer use? Unused game consoles, shoes, handbags, clothing, and jewelry can all be sold on eBay. Do you have a lot of books that you no longer read or just take up precious space? You can sell those at the local second-hand bookstore. How many watches do you have? Maybe you have a baseball card collection that's just gathering dust. You'd be surprised at how much stuff you have that you can turn into quick cash.

Look into odd jobs. If you want to save $1,000, consider working a part-time job for a couple of months. You could drive for Uber or Lyft on the weekends and make decent money. You could walk people's dogs, housesit, babysit, or even tutor (there are several websites for all of those). Do you have special skills that people could hire you for? There are a lot of freelancing opportunities on the internet.

Your home or apartment can also make you money. Do you have an extra bedroom in your home that sits empty? You could post that on a site like Airbnb. You could rent out your entire apartment or home on Airbnb for a month and stay with friends or family. $100 per night = $3,000 per month. It would be a short-term inconvenience, but you can raise a lot of money that way. Check your local laws first, because short-term rentals are not allowed everywhere.

CREDIT

How's your credit score? If you don't have any cash saved to start your business, you may need to obtain a credit card or a small loan to help you get started. Obtaining a credit card will be easier than getting a small business loan. For personal loans, lenders will want to see that your business has a history of sales first. So if you don't have the sales yet or if they're still low, your best option in the beginning will be a credit card.

Personally, I do not like debt or paying interest. I prefer to run my business on cash and direct income. But, I decided that it was time to obtain a business credit card for further security for my Etsy business. I needed access to more capital than I had in my account. If you can run your business on cash, that's ideal, but there's a good chance that you will need access to additional funding at some point.

Check your credit score. There are websites that offer free credit reports once every 12 months. You can also enroll in credit report updates, which I recommend doing right away. It's good to know what your credit score is all of the time, not just once per year.

Staying on top of your credit score is a smart move if you are starting a business. Even if you don't plan to seek out money right now, you may need to apply for a credit card or a loan within the first few months. If you know your score and can take steps now to improve it, this will benefit you down the road.

LINE OF CREDIT

Once you have been in business for a while, you may need more capital for daily operations, especially during any slow period. A line of credit will help with inventory, payroll, short-term debts, and operating expenses. You can seek out a line of credit from a bank or an online lender like Kabbage. Kabbage offers lines of credit ranging from $2,000 all the way up to $250,000.

A line of credit is the total amount that you qualify for. A loan is the amount that you withdraw from the line of credit. Each time you draw from your line of credit, a new loan is created. Each draw is a separate loan and you only pay fees on the loan or loans, not the line of credit.

Loans are paid in six or 12-month installments. Kabbage loans charge a monthly fee, and this is not based on a traditional APR. There is no penalty for early payback, there are no loan origination fees, documentation fees, or maintenance fees. If you need capital, I would recommend looking into a line of credit versus using a credit card that could have a very high interest rate.

BOOKKEEPING

Have a bookkeeping system in place before you start selling your products. Etsy will handle the online order-taking, and they will send you an annual tax form, but you need your own system to track your expenses. Even if you plan to hire a CPA to assist you with the taxes, you will need to provide the CPA with that information. You have to keep track of your spending, your car mileage, gas receipts, utility bills, business travel expenses and more.

As a home-based business, you may be able to deduct certain expenses. Keep a detailed account of what you spend on internet, home phone and cellphone. If you use one room in your house specifically for your business, you may be able to deduct a portion of your utilities, insurance, mortgage interest, property taxes, as well as depreciation. Home office deduction rules are complex and can change from year to year, so you will want to speak with a tax professional.

Look online for bookkeeping software. There are cloud-based programs, and there's software that you can download. Most programs are monthly subscriptions. QuickBooks is highly rated, and Etsy offers it on their site in the Finances section. You can get the QuickBooks and TurboTax bundle offered by Etsy for about $12 per month.

PAYMENT APPS

Be prepared to take an order outside the Etsy platform. Not every customer will want to buy from you through your Etsy shop. For whatever reason, some people just want to pay you via PayPal, Venmo, or through a different payment app. For in-person sales, Etsy uses an app called Square (read below).

Payment apps are becoming increasingly popular. Apps like PayPal, Square, Venmo, and Zelle are the bigger ones in the market. You can download these on your phone's app store and sync them to your bank account. It's very easy and inexpensive. Be prepared for these external payment requests ahead of time, because you're likely to get the occasional message on Etsy asking if you accept orders via a payment app.

Etsy has partnered with Square for in-person sales. Once you sign up for Square, they will send you a magnetic stripe reader for debit and credit cards that connects to your cellphone. Square will sync with your Etsy shop inventory, too. If you plan to make a lot of in-person sales, sign up for Square.

LOCAL MARKETS AND SHOPS

It might be tempting to market your products locally at a market, pop-up shop, or retail store. While that can be fun and getting your work out in the local community can be rewarding, you need to ask yourself if it's worth the time and money. Every hour and dollar you put into hyper-local marketing could be put toward mass marketing on Etsy and social media.

Let's say that you get approached by a local flea market to sell your work. The booth will likely cost you $100 or more. You will need a display, table, and possibly a tent. If it's a weekend event, you will have to drop everything that you're doing and spend most of your day there. While at the flea market, you won't be making new product, and you won't be paying much attention to your Etsy shop.

The weekend flea market might be fun, and you may be able to sell some items, but is it ultimately worth your time and money? Will the $500 you spend in cash and your time see dividends? Probably not. Would you be better off putting that money toward online advertising for an entire month? Probably.

$500 in Etsy and social media promotion can go a long way. I spend an average $100 per week in Facebook and Instagram advertising, and I receive at least 5,000 interactions per week. How many interactions will you get at a local flea market or pop-up shop? How many of those people will actually buy something? Think twice before spending your time and money on hyper-local promotion.

DON'T SIGN THAT LEASE

For most entrepreneurs, having an office or warehouse with your company name on the building is a life-long goal. It's something many people aspire to achieve. Perhaps it's a dream that you may have always had. That dream, however, is usually really expensive.

Work from your home for as long as you possibly can. I went through the phase of daydreaming about leasing an industrial space. I looked at them online and thought about how great it would be to have an office with a desk, a break room, and maybe even a dart board. My logo would be on the wall, with a photo of my dog on the shelf, and a water cooler in the corner.

I came to my senses after doing additional research. Not only would I have to sign a lease and pay rent every month, I would be locked into the agreement for at least one year. I'd have to pay first and last month's rent, plus a security deposit. Then add in payment for water, trash, electric, phone, and internet, as well as liability insurance. All of these require a deposit, too. Then I'd have to consider a city permit or a business license, and the city may require an inspection. That $900 per month lease quickly escalates to $1,500 or more. Every dollar you spend needlessly is a dollar that you could have pocketed.

If you absolutely need somewhere to work and cannot do it at your home, explore other options. Maybe you can rent month-to-month without being locked into an annual lease. Maybe your best friend's cousin has a two-car garage that he could rent to you. Whatever the case specific to yours, explore your options before signing a lease that you might regret or can't afford in the long-run.

DON'T OVERSPEND

You don't want to get into the position of overspending for materials one week and then needing a certain amount of sales to come in the following week to cover the previous week's spending. On Etsy, you receive orders, and the money accrues in your Etsy account. The money is then deposited into your bank account once per week, typically on Mondays. You also have the option to have the money deposited earlier, if needed.

When things are going well and sales are strong, it's a great feeling when that money goes into your bank account. When sales are slow and your Etsy account is smaller than before, it's not such a great feeling. You need to be aware that not every week is going to be the same. There will inevitably be slow weeks, and that usually happens when you least expect it.

Be careful not to overspend when everything is going well and the money is flowing in. Don't buy 500 carboard boxes this week, for example, if you only need 100 for the entire month. Don't buy 10 gallons of paint if you only need one gallon. It's tempting to get the bulk discount, but it's better to only purchase what you need on a weekly basis. Until you have a longer sales history, you should be conservative with your spending.

ETSY FEES

Etsy does not charge a monthly fee or membership fee, but there are a number of other fees to keep in mind. The fees you pay as a shop owner are below:

- Listing fee: If you list items for sale, you will pay a listing fee, which is currently 20 cents per item. All listings expire, and you have to manually renew them or set up automatic renewal. Once a listing is renewed, you will be charged 20 cents again.
- Selling fee: If an item sells, you will pay a seller's fee. Currently, the fee is 5%.
- Payment processing fee: These vary depending on the country you are in. In the United States, the fee is currently 3% and 25 cents per transaction. There are currency conversion fees as well.
- Transaction charge: If someone in another country buys your item in a different currency, you will pay a 2.5% transaction charge.
- There are also fees if you decide to implement Etsy's shopping engine ads and promoted listings. Etsy also charges fees if you

implement their abandoned cart and recently favorited campaigns. Before setting up any Etsy promotion, read about their fees and make sure that you have a budget set.

PASSIVE INCOME

You have probably heard the financial term "passive income." Passive income is money earned on a regular basis that requires little to no effort by the recipient. Examples of passive income are money earned via rental property, royalty payments, or earning money from a business that you are invested in but do not participate in the operations.

Etsy sellers are actively involved in the creation of products and the business itself, so running an Etsy shop is not a passive income source. However, there are ways to make your Etsy business more passive and less active. One such way is to utilize an Etsy production partner.

When you use a production partner, you act as the designer of the product(s) while the production partner does the manufacturing. In many cases, the production partner can also drop ship the products. Drop shipping is when the manufacturer ships the product directly to the customer instead of shipping to you, the designer. Drop shipping takes the hassle of shipping off your plate.

Another way to have a more passive Etsy business is to utilize automation. Think 3D printing: whether you do the 3D printing at home or use a production partner to do it for you, you will still be creating products passively. You will have to design the product and set up the printer, but you are passing along the actual production to a machine. This will save you a lot of time in the long-term.

As 3D printing technology evolves and becomes less expensive, expect to see more Etsy shops churning out 3D printed products. There are already shops that sell 3D printed home goods, jewelry, toys, and gadgets. If you are not great at making things with your hands but are good with designing and technology, having a shop that sells 3D printed products may be the right choice for you.

$100,000+ PER YEAR

I didn't start off on Etsy making $100,000+ per year in revenue. It took time and hard work. For the first year, my shop was a part-time hobby, and I was only selling a couple of items per month. By changing my focus and adding different products and new listings, I was able to increase my sales quickly dramatically. My part-time Etsy hobby evolved into a full-time business in the span of just one month.

You may not want a full-time Etsy business. Maybe you're doing this part-time to supplement your income or simply because you enjoy it. You can have a part-time Etsy business, but there is always a chance that it could turn into a full-time operation. Be prepared to receive more orders than you initially anticipated in case your shop really does take off.

You can make $100,000+ per year in revenue on Etsy. If you're selling $10 t-shirts, you will need to sell an average of 834 shirts per month to reach that level of revenue per year. If you're selling $50 pairs of shoes, you will need to sell 167 pairs of shoes per month. Basically, if your goal is to make $100,000 per year, figure out how much product you will need to sell to reach your goal. Whatever your goal is, as long as you put in the time and energy required, there's a good chance that you can achieve success on Etsy.

DELUSIONS OF GRANDEUR

Don't let a little success go to your head. It's easy to have one great month and start dreaming about buying a new car or planning a trip to Europe. If you can afford those things, that's great. But, if you're a new business, and you don't have a financial track record to refer to yet, it's best to play it safe and save some money for when sales aren't so high. Slower months are inevitable, and you will need cash to get through those slower periods.

Your Etsy business isn't a normal job where you can expect a certain amount of money to go into your bank account every week. One month could be amazing, and the next month could be slow. For my business, summer was slow while the rest of the year was great. I didn't know that would be the case, but the workflow was pretty consistent. After a year or two in business, you can look back and view the sales trends and project for the future.

I'm not telling you not to enjoy your success. It's best, however, to prepare for the financial roller coaster that can come with running your own business. There will be ups and downs. If you can stay grounded and not spend all of the profits, you will be in good shape during the slow periods.

BECOME A LLC

If your Etsy business takes off and becomes your primary source of income, you may want to consider making your business a Limited Liability Company (LLC). Becoming an LLC protects its members (you and any partners you work with) from personal liability. Like a corporation, its members receive liability protection from any debts and lawsuits. Each state has different laws that determine any tax benefits and liability protection.

One main advantage of forming an LLC is to avoid the high self-employment tax. If you are a sole proprietor or partnership and not operating as an LLC, the federal self-employment tax rate is currently 15.3% on the first $132,900 of net income plus 2.9% on any income in excess of $132,900. Depending on your income and the state in which you reside, you could benefit from forming an LLC.

I would not recommend filing to become an LLC on your own. The IRS has strict guidelines, and each state has different rules. The rules and guidelines could change. Be sure to meet with an attorney before filing your LLC paperwork.

TWO SHOPS ARE BETTER THAN ONE?

When my shop started to become successful, I began to consider opening a second shop. The new shop would sell similar items, but with a different aesthetic. It would target the same customers but those with different tastes. Why not have two shops and make even more money, right? To me, having two Etsy shops seemed like a great idea.

Consider how difficult it would be to run two different shops at the same time. How will you manage an entirely new shop and keep your existing shop running smoothly? Can you handle the added workload? Can you keep up with order fulfillment if both shops are successful?

I ultimately didn't end up launching the second shop, and I'm thankful that I didn't. I was already working six days per week. I decided that I could not handle double the orders if the new shop were to succeed. I was already near my maximum output. If I had a second shop, I would need to hire additional help. I decided to instead focus on making my existing shop the best that it could be.

Chapter 3 – Products

YOUR PRODUCTS

What are you going to sell? You may already know the answer, but if not, you can browse Etsy for inspiration. There are thousands of product options. Searching Etsy's offerings is a great way to do your initial research and get inspiration for your own business.

As far as having a successful Etsy shop, it is a good idea to offer more than one type of product. As per my previous example, if you only sell yoga mats, people that are searching for yoga bags or yoga balls will probably not find your mats. They might eventually find your shop, but "yoga mats" is a very specific search. If you can diversify your product line, you can attract more visitors, and more visitors means more sales.

What makes your product(s) unique? Is your competition doing the same exact thing as you? One way to stand out on Etsy is to create familiar products with your own personal style.

A totally new product will be harder to sell than something that is familiar. Sure, your new 3D printed gadget or hammock for dogs could be a hit, but since they don't exist yet, there's no guarantee that people will want them. If you want to create a successful shop, it's a good idea to start selling familiar products that already exist first. With time, you can add your own style or twist that makes it unique. If you want to introduce completely new products in the future, you can do that later. I would not recommend starting a new shop with unproven products.

PRODUCTION OUTPUT

How much product can you possibly make by yourself? Before you decide what type of shop you will open, you need to determine what your maximum production capability is. Your maximum production output will determine your possible order fulfillment and – most importantly – your maximum potential revenue.

If you can make a maximum of seven yoga mats per day with a profit of $15 each, that's $105 per day (then subtract for any fees and taxes). The most that you can expect to earn per day, if everything goes well, is $105. That's assuming that you can sell all seven mats in that one day.

If you can make seven per day, but you sell 10 yoga mats per day, you will have a problem fulfilling those orders by yourself. You may have to hire part-time help to assist with production. Then, you also have to consider the cost of the help and the profit you are making. If part-time help increases your output but reduces your profit, then you may need to raise your prices to help cover the additional cost.

You can only produce so much by yourself. Knowing what your maximum output is in the beginning will help you plan for a future when you may need to hire help. At the same time, you don't want to spend half of your profit on hiring help. If your profit margin is too slim, you may not be in the position of being able to hire someone to assist you.

FINANCIAL SENSE

Does the product make sense financially? Let's say that a yoga mat takes one hour to produce and costs you $25 in materials and time. A pair of sandals takes 30 minutes to produce and costs you $20 in materials and time. The yoga mat sells for $40, and the sandals also sell for $40. In an eight-hour day, you can only produce eight yoga mats.

For eight yoga mats, revenue would be $320 and potential profit is $105. In the same eight-hour day, you can produce 16 pairs of sandals. Revenue on the sandals would be $640, and the potential profit is $320.

You can double the revenue and triple the profit by adding in the production of the sandals. Wouldn't you rather put the same amount of time and energy into earning $320 per day instead of earning only $105? You might really enjoy making yoga mats, but also making sandals makes the most financial sense.

There's only so much time in one day, and you can only produce so much. You want to get the most out of your time as well as your potential output. As much as you might enjoy making something, sometimes it doesn't make sense financially. Before creating any new product, take the time to figure out your maximum output and greatest potential profit. Don't blindly produce products without knowing your cost in time and money.

PRICING YOUR PRODUCTS

Before I priced my products, I did my research. I looked at the competition and examined their pricing in detail. From there, I figured out what my production and selling costs would be and what I expected my profit to be.

Can you be competitive and still make a profit? Etsy is a competitive marketplace where most customers do a lot of product comparison and price shopping. If your product is 10% more expensive and appears to be about the same quality as the other guy, then there's a good chance that you might lose sales. If your product is a little more expensive but appears to be better quality, you could win over a lot of customers.

Don't price your items low just to undercut your competition. Make sure that you can still make a profit at that price point. Remember that Etsy will take its percentage from any sale and there will be credit card processing fees, too. Currently, Etsy seller fees and credit card fees total approximately 10% of any sale. You also need to factor in taxes because you'll be expected to pay those later.

When pricing your items, figure your cost + fees + taxes, and then set your price. Let's say something cost you $10 to produce, and you want to price it at $20. Your profit will be $10 minus fees and taxes. Etsy seller fees and credit card processing will be about 10% ($2), and federal income tax will be about 25% ($5). That's $7 in fees and taxes. Your actual profit is $3 ($20 - $7 = $13). Your tax rate will depend on your filing status, business structure and state of residence.

PRODUCT OPTIONS

One reason my shop succeeded is because I let my customers customize their tables. Most furniture shops on Etsy at the time only offered people a few color or style choices. I saw that opportunity and decided to offer 15 stain colors and 15 paint colors, and additionally, people could select a custom paint color for just $25 more.

Most people like being part of the design process, especially on Etsy, even if it's just being able to pick colors. If you can offer different options, whether it's color or design or size, it will benefit you. At the same time, you do not want to make it too complicated for the customer.

Don't have one product listing that is available in 15 sizes, 20 shapes, and 25 colors because that could get very confusing. If you need to create 50 different listings to make it less confusing, then do that instead. Try to find the right balance of customization and simplification. If your listings are too confusing and there are too many options, the customer might get discouraged and leave your shop.

UPDATING PRODUCTS

Update your product listings on a regular basis. Some products will sell better than others. Make sure that you review your listings on a monthly basis, if not weekly. The first of the month is a good time to review and update your listings.

If a product isn't selling after 30 days of listing it, you should look into the reasons why. Revisit the tag words and see if there are different words that might work better for that item. Perhaps it's time to update the item's photo. If the tag words and photos don't seem to be the issue, maybe it's the product itself. It might be time to lower the price or remove the listing entirely.

Add new products every week or at least every month if you can. Repeat customers will expect to see new products in your shop. Get rid of the items that are not selling or place those items on sale. You can have an entire section in your shop for those items on sale. Also, when you add new items to your shop, make sure that you promote the listings on social media and in the shop's Update section.

ETSY PRODUCTION PARTNERS

If you are not a maker of a product, you can still produce items and sell them on Etsy. You can use a production partner to help you make your products. Etsy does require that you have a hand in the design process and creation of the product, but you do not have to physically produce it yourself. You can be a designer and use another business to produce your items.

A production partner, by Etsy's definition, includes but is not limited to the following services: printing, 3D printing, casting, plating, cutting and sewing, and finishing. Etsy allows you to keep the name of your production partner a secret, but you do need to disclose that you use a production partner. You should include this information in your About page as well as on your listings. Include where this partner is located and a description of the work that they do for you. Etsy may contact you for detailed information.

Etsy expects you to be honest and transparent in your business. It is best to adhere to their guidelines, as they have the right to suspend or terminate your shop if you do not respect those parameters. If you want to learn more about production partners and Etsy's guidelines, read their Terms of Use on their website. Simply put, do not sell something and claim to be the maker if you are not.

TRENDS

You don't have to be a trendsetter or a trend follower to be successful on Etsy. Trends come and go, so doing something trendy may not be the best route if you want to build a lasting business. The fidget spinner was trendy, but was it a good product for long-term success? If your shop only sold fidget spinners, what would your sales look like after one year? After two years?

When you're thinking about what to sell on Etsy, you need to consider the future. If you want your shop to be a success, you will want to offer products that have lasting appeal. As an example, items like jewelry, clothing, kitchenware, furniture, and art will always be in demand. You can offer a trendy version of something that people already want, like personalized coffee mugs, but at the same time, you may want to also offer plates, bowls, etc. to satisfy the customers that still want the basics.

If you build your shop around a trendy product, you will need to adapt to frequent change. At some point, the trend will dissipate or go away completely, so you will need to offer different products. Always be looking for new product ideas, and be ready to diversify. One way to stay current on Etsy is to follow your competition, and observe what they are doing. Use your competition for idea inspiration -- not to copy them, but to stay sharp and in-tune.

PHOTOS

The photos you include on your Etsy listings are the first images that your potential customers will see. You want your photos to be clear, well-lit, appealing, and professional. You want to make a great first impression, as these photos will either draw people in or turn them away. You don't want bad lighting and bad settings to turn people away.

If you have experience with photography and image editing, you can probably get away with taking your own photos. This is a risk because if your photos are mediocre, people will feel that your business and product is mediocre.

If you are ultimately unsure about your abilities, hire a photographer. Why risk creating an entire business that's dependent on great product images only to fail because your product images are subpar? You want to create a shop that is professional, so don't hire your buddy. Hire a professional.

You can find professional photographers online through websites like Upwork, Thumbtack, Fiverr, and Freelancer. You can do a Google search for local photographers or post an ad on Craigslist. Be sure to check out their work, their website, read the reviews, and ask to see their latest work.

NUMBER OF LISTINGS

How many product listings should you have? Some shops have 25, 50, or 100, while some shops have over 1,000. The more listings you have, the better chance that people will see your products when they search on Etsy.

The categories that your listings are in are also very important. The category is where your listing will live on Etsy's main page. The more categories your products are in, the better. If you only sell dresses, your shop of course will appear in only one category. If you sell dresses, shoes, jewelry, toys, and art, your shop will clearly appear in several categories. The more categories with which you can be associated, the more you will appear in searches.

You don't need to have 1,000 listings to be successful. You should have quality listings that display excellent photos. Your listings should maximize the use of tag words (you are allowed 13 tag words per listing). Your product descriptions should also be very easy to understand. Focus on quality over quantity.

The most listings I had at one time was around 45. I had several very popular products that accounted for 90% of my sales. My shop is proof that you don't need to have 100 or 500 product listings.

KEEP INNOVATING

Beyond the risk of starting a business, there are other risks once you open your shop. Once things are going smoothly, there's a chance that you will become comfortable. There's a chance that you will be busy and might stop innovating. Why change anything if your shop is doing well?

You don't want your shop to become stagnant or stale. You need to come up with new ideas and new products. Introduce a new item once a week or at least once a month. The new product might not be a hit, but if you continue to innovate, you will come up with even better products.

Customers who like your shop will expect you to offer new products. Existing customers are the ones who will refer you to friends, and they're the ones who will return to order more items. Not providing them with anything new will probably drive their business away.

One way to keep innovating is to keep an eye on the competition. Spend some time every month researching what your competitors are offering. You will want to know about any new products they are selling. Don't copy your competition, but seeing what they are doing is a great way to fuel your own creativity.

Chapter 4 – Marketing

MARKETING YOUR SHOP

How do you plan to let people know that your shop exists? Once your shop is live, your listings will appear in Etsy search results, but you still need to take action to drive customers directly to your shop. You should not rely solely on Etsy to market your shop. If you want to succeed, you need to understand marketing basics. For marketing a new Etsy business, I've simplified the marketing plan process below.

A marketing plan is a list of steps or actions necessary to achieve a goal.

1. Market Research – Get data on your market. Is your market growing? Who are the customers? What's the future outlook for your market?
2. Competition – Who's your competition? What will you do differently to stand out? What can you do better?
3. Strategy – What actions will you take to promote your shop? Google Ads? Facebook and Instagram promotions? YouTube? Etsy ads?
4. Budget – How much can you afford to spend to promote your shop?
5. Goals – Where do you want sales to be in six months? 12 months?
6. Results – When will you review your marketing efforts and adjust your actions? What have you learned?

Marketing an Etsy shop is mostly an online effort. Take advantage of the promotional tools that Etsy has available, and you should promote your shop on social media. If your efforts are not creating the results you want, try something else. Review your marketing plan every six or 12 months, and revise it as needed.

SOCIAL MEDIA

Use Facebook, Instagram, Pinterest, and Twitter to promote your Etsy shop. Every business should have a social media presence. Before you even open your Etsy shop, you should have social media accounts set up for your business. You may have a personal preference for using Instagram or Twitter, but you should really use all of them.

Facebook owns Instagram, so once you have accounts set up for both, you can link those together. This will make life a lot easier for you. When you post something on Instagram, you can opt-in to have it automatically post to your Facebook account. And when you create an advertisement on Facebook, you can choose to run the same ad to Instagram. One promotional campaign works for both platforms.

Pinterest is an obvious choice for promoting your products because Pinterest is all about products. Make sure that you create a Pinterest account so that when you create a new product listing on Etsy, you can share it to Pinterest. It's a remarkable promotional tool.

Twitter may not be the number one platform for promoting your Etsy shop, but you should still use it. You can have a Twitter account that is more of a behind-the-scenes account or more of a blog about you and what you like, but still utilize it to promote your shop. Get creative with Twitter and find out how you can make it work for your promotional needs. Your Twitter doesn't have to promote the same content as your Facebook and Instagram.

TARGET MARKET

Who is your target customer? When you think about your shop and your products, who do you picture as the buyer? Is it men, women, or both? What is their average age? Where do they live? What are their interests?

Let's use the yoga mat scenario again in this target market study. According to the website thegoodbody.com, 36 million people in the U.S. practice yoga. 72 percent of those are female, and most of them are between 30 and 49. 75 percent of yogis also participate in other sports. $16 billion is spent every year on yoga classes, equipment, and related products.*

From these general statistics, you can see that yoga is a big business. Most people doing yoga are female, but the number of male participants is increasing. The number of men practicing yoga in 2016 was 10 million. If your shop only sells products that target women, you may want to rethink that approach. You might be able to create a niche product that will be popular with both men and women.

Before you set up your shop, do some research into your potential target market. It took me two minutes to search for those yoga statistics online. It's valuable information, and it was free. Of course, you should verify any information that you discover online and double check the facts.

*The Good Body, November 16, 2018 www.thegoodbody.com/yoga-statistics/

MARKET SIZE

How many potential customers are there for your products? Do you sell products for children, men, women, both men and women? If you are making toys only for children aged 0-3, your potential market size will be much smaller than if you are also making hats for children and adults in addition to the toys, for example.

How crowded is your product category on Etsy? Take a look at how many competitors you will have just on Etsy alone. If you are producing yoga mats, you should familiarize yourself with the competition. If your shop is one of two shops selling yoga mats, for example, your potential Etsy Market Share would be 50%.

Before opening a new shop, make sure that you won't be competing against 500 other shops that are making very similar products. If so, your potential market share will be small. If this is the case, you may want to reconsider your product offerings. Think of different products or ways that will make your products unique, whether it be the design, color, customization opportunities, etc.

PROMOTED LISTINGS

Once you create your listings, you can decide if you want to promote them on Etsy. Promoted listings are chosen by you that you pay to have featured within the Etsy search platform.

If your shop is new and you want to get more traffic, I would suggest promoting some of your listings. Make sure that the listing itself is complete before promoting it. Check that you've filled out the tag words, description, shipping information, etc. If the listing is not complete, it may not rank high when people search.

Set a reasonable budget. Promoted listings are an extra expense, and your account will be charged accordingly. Instead of promoting all of your listings, start with a few and monitor the campaign to see how they perform. After a week or two, you will see results and may want to add to or cancel some of the promotions.

You will have to decide on your maximum daily budget for ad spending. $1 per day is the lowest you can set it at, but I recommend setting a budget of at least $5 per day and monitor the results for one week. After seven days, you can decide if you want to continue as is or make changes. You can edit, pause, or cancel the campaign at any time.

ABANDONED CART AND RECENTLY FAVORITED

A newer feature on Etsy is the Abandoned Cart and Recently Favorited promotional campaigns. You will find these in the Sales and Coupons section. These are separate marketing campaigns that you have to activate. Etsy will not run these campaigns unless you set them up.

The Abandoned Cart campaign will automatically send potential customers a coupon if they leave your items in their cart. You determine the coupon type (i.e., 10% off or $5 off) and select your budget. The current cost to you is 10 cents per coupon sent. You can set a budget of $5.00 per month, $10, $20, etc. or unlimited (which is recommended by Etsy). Etsy will then automatically send your coupon to these people with abandoned carts, and you don't have to do anything once it is set up.

The Recently Favorited campaign is almost the same exact thing, but Etsy will send the coupon to people that have favorited your items. I would recommend setting up both of these campaigns. Once customers catch on to this, some people will deliberately leave items in their carts or favorite an item because they are hoping to receive a coupon. If you don't set up these campaigns, people won't receive a coupon from you.

Etsy also shares your campaign's performance with you so you will be able to see how many people order because of these campaigns. 10 cents per coupon sent is a small amount to pay Etsy to help you generate additional sales.

CREATE COUPON CODES

Creating a coupon code is different than having a sale. When you have a sale, you select the items to be included in the sale, and the listings will then show that they have been reduced in price. When you create a coupon code, however, the customer needs to enter the code at checkout.

A coupon code is a great way to promote your shop on social media or elsewhere. You can create a special discount with a coupon code for your followers on Facebook, for example. Then, on Facebook, tell people about the coupon code. This way, your followers will feel that they are receiving a special deal only for Facebook followers. When someone uses that code during the checkout process, you will know that they saw it on Facebook.

You can have several different coupon codes at the same time that can have different discounts. I have a 10% off coupon code only for existing customers. I include a thank you card with every item shipped, and the code is printed on the card. It is a way to encourage repeat business, and it's also a way to track repeat customers to see if they use the code and from what platform or strategy they received it.

HAVE A SALE

Are you new to Etsy and want to draw attention to your shop? Is it the middle of summer and sales are slow? Is it Monday and you want to start the week off strong? Have a sale!

Putting your entire shop on sale is a great way to increase traffic. You can have a sale whenever you want to. If you want to celebrate Speak Like A Pirate Day, then have a sale. It's totally up to you.

When you create a sale, you select the discount amount, which listings to include, and the duration of the sale. July and August are typically my slower months, so I create a 10% off sale during these months to help stimulate traffic. The great thing is that people see your listing, and the first thing they notice is that the price is marked down. That generates more interest in your listing, and people are more likely to click on it.

If your competitor is having a sale on Etsy, you may want to do the same. Try to stay aware of your competition and what they are doing. Also, keep track of the major shopping holidays.

HOLIDAY SALES

Plan ahead for holiday sales, not only with your inventory, but for your holiday marketing. Will you run holiday-themed ads on Instagram and Facebook? Will you create some new listings for the holiday? Should you temporarily change your banner image?

Keep track of the big shopping holidays because your competition will do so. In the U.S., Thanksgiving, Christmas, Black Friday, Cyber Monday, Small Business Saturday, and Hanukkah all fall within a month of each other. You can try to acknowledge each holiday, or you can put your entire shop on sale for one month. I personally recommend the latter.

You can increase your following and sales if you appeal to a broader audience. If many of your customers reside in Canada, for example, you may want to familiarize yourself with their own biggest holidays. What is Boxing Day in Canada, and should you celebrate it on Etsy? If a large percentage of your sales are to other countries, learn more about those countries and their holiday traditions.

SHARE YOUR 5-STAR REVIEWS

Your 5-star reviews are another incredible marketing tool. Your happiest customers will often give you a glowing review and may even include a note and photo. Don't be shy or reserved in sharing these. You should be proud of your great reviews, and you should share them on social media.

Potential customers trust what your existing customers have to say about you and your products. People are more likely to buy from you if you have happy customers that had a great experience with your shop. Those who give you a 5-star review are normally the ones who LOVE your product as well as your customer service. If you can, share the reviews that include a note about their experience.

On Etsy, the social media tool is in the Marketing section. Here, you can share your 5-star reviews by clicking on the "social accounts" and link to your Facebook, Instagram, Pinterest, or Twitter accounts. Share a 5-star review at least once per week.

CELEBRATE MILESTONES

Celebrate your shop's success. You can use your milestones for marketing and promotion. When you hit the 100 sales mark, for example, let everyone know. Celebrate by having a weekend sale and post the news on social media. "We just hit 100 sales! Celebrate with us!"

Milestones can be anything that you care to share with people, whether it's the number of sales, number of followers, number of listing favorites, etc. Celebrate within the Etsy community as well, as it's a very supportive space with other users supporting others. People will follow you on Etsy, so you should post in the Update section and use your milestones to help increase your business.

STAND OUT FROM THE CROWD

You want your shop to stand out, right? There's a lot of competition on Etsy, so do your best to create a shop that is both interesting and unique. Here are some ideas on how to make your shop stand out:

- Banner Image - Create a unique look for your shop.
- Logo – Create a shop logo. If you need help creating a logo, look online for a graphic artist. There are freelance artists who can create an inexpensive logo for you.
- Main photos – Get creative with your photos. Add a small watermark to the corner of every main photo. The watermark can be your logo, a symbol, a thumbs up, a smiley face, or whatever you want it to be. Most photos on Etsy do not have a watermark, so this can help you stand out.
- Highlight photos – Add a bright outline to your photos. A red or yellow outline around your main photo will help it stand out from the rest.
- Hire a photographer – Professional photos are much better than mediocre photos. Yes, the iPhone has a great camera, but that doesn't mean that you are a great product photographer.
- Sale – Want to get noticed? Have a sale. If you look at most listings on Etsy, they are regular priced. When you have a sale, the listing stands out because the new price is highlighted. It's a good way to catch someone's attention.

INCLUDE A FREE GIFT

One way to thank your customers and show them that you appreciate their business is to include a free gift. Many sellers on Etsy subscribe to this practice, and it's usually just something small and handmade. People love receiving free gifts.

If you can include a gift, that's great. If you are selling $5 pairs of socks, you probably don't need to include a gift. The low selling price doesn't really justify including a gift. But, if you are selling items that are $50 or $100, for example, that might warrant including a gift that's worth a couple of dollars. A free gift can be something small that you made, like a keychain, bottle opener or bracelet. The theme of your shop will likely dictate the type of gift you give.

When I ship my coffee tables, I include free drink coasters. I wrap the cork coasters with a paper ribbon that has my logo on it. The coasters cost me about 25 cents each. They look nice and they are a thoughtful, useful gift.

You may not be able to afford giving away any gifts, and that's okay. I would recommend sending your customer a thank you card and/or a card with a coupon code they can use with their next purchase. You want to tell them that you appreciate their business and encourage them to order from your shop again. A simple card is an inexpensive way to get that message across to your valued customer.

BUSINESS CARDS

Business cards are an inexpensive marketing tool. My business card is very simple: my logo is on one side, and my website's domain is on the other. I keep some in my car and some in my wallet. You'd be surprised at how often people ask me what I do. It's usually a stranger in line at the store or a person working the register, but I always have a business card on hand just in case. You never know who could be a potential customer.

Another practice I've adopted is to include a business card with every order I ship. If the customer is happy with your product, there's a good chance that they will refer you or share your card with a friend, relative, or neighbor. Even if they don't, it's a nice reminder to the customer that you are a real business, and they'll know where to look if they want to order from you again.

You can also customize a business card to encourage repeat business. I have a second version of business cards that I only send to existing customers. My logo is on one side, and I include a coupon code on the other side: "Thank you for your order. Use this code to receive 10% off your next order." Existing customers are the people who will order again, especially if they love your product and you offer them a discount. The $20 I spent to create those 500 business cards has been well worth it. Think of ways that you can get creative using business cards. It's an inexpensive marketing tool that can increase your sales and generate awareness of your brand.

FACEBOOK AND INSTAGRAM ADS

It's also recommended to advertise on Facebook and Instagram at the same time. Facebook owns Instagram, so when you have accounts on both Facebook and Instagram, you can link the two accounts. Then, when you advertise on Facebook, you can choose to run that same ad on Instagram.

Ads on Facebook are easy to do once your Facebook page is changed to a business page. These ads are called "promotions." First, create a post as you would normally do. Add a photo and text, then simply post it. You will see the "boost" button on the bottom corner. That's where you want to click to promote that post.

Once you click "boost," you will be able to choose your target market (i.e., men and women in the United States between 18 and 40 who like surfing, skiing, art, dogs, and pizza). You will also set your budget and promotion duration. If you want to run the ad on Instagram and you already linked the two accounts, then all you have to do is click the box next to "run promotion on Instagram."

Once your promotion is approved, which is usually within a few minutes, your promotion will be live. You can promote several posts at a time, or just one at a time. You can spend anywhere from $5 per day or $100 per day -- it's up to you. Your credit card will be charged after the promotion ends. I recommend to start off by promoting one post for one week. After seven days, view the results and see how it performed.

USE FACEBOOK TO TEST PRODUCTS

Facebook is a great tool for marketing, but you can also use it to test your products and pricing. Before posting a new product to Etsy, ask your Facebook network what they think of it. Post a photo or two and a short description of the item. Ask people what they would expect to pay. You will get some helpful feedback, and it's free market research.

You can use Facebook to see what people actually think of your products. Ask people for their honest opinion. Some of your Facebook friends will be nice, of course, because they don't want to hurt your feelings. Others will be totally honest with you, especially if you don't know them very well.

Getting people's opinions before going to market is just smart research on your part. You may not want to open yourself up to any criticism, but look at it as market research. You are most likely emotionally invested in your idea or product that it may be hard for you to view it with a critical eye. To be in business and succeed, you need to be able to accept constructive criticism without taking it personal.

FACEBOOK POLLS

When you create a post on Facebook, you have the option of making a poll. A poll can be a great way to test out a new product, design, or idea within your community.

Use the poll feature to get people's opinion on something. "Which color do you like best? A or B?" or "Which design do you like? A, B, or C?" You can also ask people about pricing: "What would you pay for this item? $19.00? $25.00? $29.00?"

While polling on Facebook may not get you the most accurate results, it enables you to interact with your immediate audience. It's also a great way to promote your business, and it can be fun, too. People usually like Facebook posts that asks for their opinion on something.

FACEBOOK LIVE

Use Facebook Live to engage your existing and potential customers.

The thought of doing live video streaming makes most people nervous. Before going live, be sure to rehearse what you plan to say, and make some notes if you need to. Have a few key talking points, and know ahead of time how you will end the video: "Thanks for watching! Contact me any time and visit my Etsy shop! Have a great day!" Be upbeat and make it fun. Keep your Facebook Live between two and three minutes.

Use Facbeook Live to update people about new products, show people behind the scenes where you produce the items, or announce an upcoming sale. You can also have a secret coupon code just for Facebook Live viewers. People always enjoy receiving a special discount. Be creative with your videos, and use them to promote your business in a fun, new way.

PINTEREST

Pinterest is an image-based social media platform that is perfect for promoting your Etsy business. If you don't use Pinterest, do yourself a favor and download the app on your phone and create an account. Start posting photos from your Etsy shop, and create a "board" for your shop and post photos to it as often as you can.

On Etsy, you can see where your shop visitors are coming from, whether it's from search or your social media efforts. Most of my social media visitors came from Pinterest, which surprised me because I wasn't advertising on Pinterest at the time. Other people were posting my product photos to Pinterest, and people were finding my Etsy shop from there. Don't leave it to random people to do the work for you, though. Once I discovered this, I started promoting on Pinterest.

Pinterest has over 250 million active users per month. It's not as big as Facebook or Instagram, but Pinterest is a huge platform where people are looking for new and interesting products, ideas, design, art, clothing, crafts, etc. You can also advertise on Pinterest the same way as Facebook and Instagram.

GOOGLE ADS

In addition to social media marketing, you can run your own ad campaign with Google Ads (formerly called AdWords). Advertising with Google is simple, and you can easily choose your budget and select the type of campaign you want to run. You can target your city, state, region, the entire country, or even multiple countries.

First, go to their website (ads.google.com) and set up your free account. You only pay for the campaigns that you run. I would recommend starting out with just one ad campaign to get comfortable with the process. Create the campaign, set a budget, and then keep an eye on your campaign. After a week or two, you can see how your ad campaign is performing and decide if you want to edit it, stop it, or create another campaign.

Google Ads makes it easy to edit your ads. You can edit your ad at any time and there is no fee for stopping your ad early. The most important thing you want to do is check how your ad is performing. Make changes, if necessary, or try one of their other ad types. They offer search ads, display, video, and app ads.

HIRE A MARKETING EXPERT

You might not want to do the marketing by yourself. You might be too busy making product or you just might not want to deal with it. If you can afford to hire a marketing professional to help with part or all of your marketing efforts, that would be a wise decision. Not only will it take some responsibility off your plate, it will help free up your time.

Marketing agencies exist throughout the country. There are national agencies, which will be very expensive to hire, and there are small ones in every major city. I would recommend performing a Yelp search and find a small agency near you that has good reviews. You can also search for freelance professionals on sites like Upwork and Fiverr. A freelancer will be more affordable than hiring an agency.

Many marketing agencies and freelancers also offer design and website services. If you want to hire them to help you create a logo, website, SEO, and do your social media marketing, you can. Or, you can just hire them to handle your social media campaigns. It all depends on your budget. At some point, if you can afford to spend a few hundred dollars or more per month on marketing, consider hiring a professional.

Chapter 5 – Website

CREATE A WEBSITE

Should you have a website? Definitely. Every business in today's world should have a website, and your Etsy shop is absolutely a business. Have you ever searched for a company and didn't find their website? When that happens to me, I usually think, "well, this isn't a real business."

You can create a basic website inexpensively. I used a website building platform called Weebly to create my site, and I've been using Weebly for years. You can register your domain name and have a basic website online the same day you sign up. Etsy offers a similar platform called Pattern (see below).

It's best to start with a basic website. Upload some product photos, have an "about" page, include a contact form, and add the link to your Etsy shop. Make sure that you also implement the SEO (search engine optimization) and keywords, *as your main goal is to drive traffic to your Etsy shop.*

As I mentioned, Etsy has its own website building platform called Pattern. With Pattern, you can create a website very easily and inexpensively and automatically sync and integrate your Etsy shop. You can set up a domain name, select a theme, and edit your information in minutes. With Pattern, there's no excuse not to have a website.

DOMAIN NAME

A domain name is your website address (i.e., www.101etsytips.com).
How do you choose a domain name? Ideally, it's recommended that
your name is ten characters or less. As you can imagine, most domain
names that you brainstorm will probably already be taken and
registered. As a result, you will need to get creative to come up with
something original.

People have a hard time remembering long domain names, and search
engines rank longer domains lower. A name like
www.susanstotallyawesomegifts.com is just too long, and nobody
wants to type that into the search bar. Keep it as short as possible.

Get a .com or .co if you can. Search engines like Google reportedly
give precedence to domains that are top-tier (.com, .org, .co). Names
that have second-tier extensions (.biz, .me, .mobi) will receive second-
tier placement. You don't have to have a top-level name with the .com
-- it can be .biz or .me, but your name should be 10 characters or less,
if possible.

SEO

Search engine optimization (SEO) is setting up your website's
keywords and text so that your site appears in relevant online searches.
Every search engine, like Google, uses algorithms to sort and rank
websites according to keywords. You ideally want to get traffic to your
site, so you need to create a destination that is rich in relevant content.

When you are creating the text for your website, think about keywords
plus content. Think about the way a customer will search for your
product. Will they type in "yoga mat" or "yoga gear" or "rubber yoga
mat" or "exercise mat"? Come up with 20-30 keywords that a

customer would use when searching for your items. You can look at similar listings on Etsy and see which words your competitors are using. The tag words they use will be visible at the bottom of the listing.

Once you have the 20-30 keywords that you think are the best for your products, use those words throughout your website -- not just in product listings, but in the copy of the website. Don't just use "Yoga Mat" in your product headline. Be more descriptive. Example: "Black yoga mat with flowers and bird" and "Blue yoga mat with red rose." If you believe that your customers are searching for specific colors, shapes, styles, or materials, use those words in your listing headline and product description.

LINK LIKE CRAZY

Linking is inserting a hyperlink from one webpage to another. When you click on a news headline, for example, and the article opens in a different window on a different website, that's a link.

You can increase your website's ranking in search engines if you have more links connecting to your site. If there are 50 links, for example, from other websites pointing to your website with "yoga mat" in the text (called "anchor text"), your site will rank higher in search results. In other words, you want more websites to link to your website.

Here are some ways that you can increase your links:

1. Do your own linking (Etsy shop to website and vice versa)
2. If your friends and family have a website, ask them to link to yours
3. Create a press release and get blogs and news sites to link to your site

4. Contact blogs or sites that might be interested in link sharing

5. Link your social media accounts to your shop and website

You also want to link internally on Etsy. When you create a new listing, you can create a link to another listing in your shop in the product description. Cross-linking within your shop helps search engines define that your shop is related. Don't forget to create links from your website to your Etsy shop and its listings. Create a new link every week or so to remain fresh with search engines. Search engines are constantly changing their algorithms, so try to stay current with any changes that may affect your business.

Chapter 6 – Get Help

HIRING

The thought of hiring someone can be daunting. You may not need the help in the beginning, but if your business becomes full-time, it may become necessary. I tried to do everything myself until I couldn't. I became too busy and had so many orders that I knew that I needed help.

If you can find a friend or relative who's willing to volunteer their time to help you, I would explore that option first. If that doesn't work, use your network of friends and family to find a reliable assistant. I was able to hire my mother-in-law's boyfriend. He was retired and was interested in doing some woodworking part-time.

Don't start off by hiring someone full-time. Hire someone part-time and have them fill out a W9 tax form. For tax purposes, a 1099 employee is considered an independent contractor. Independent contractors provide services to companies, like yours, meaning they are not actual employees. They will get paid by you, but they will need to save part of their earnings to pay their income tax.

DON'T PAY IN CASH

You could pay someone under the table to help you, but I would not recommend doing this. It might be easier to pay someone cash and not have to worry about taxes, but you will not be able to deduct any of that from your income. If you pay someone $5,000 in cash per year under the table, that's $5,000 that you cannot deduct. You lose out, and they don't have to pay any income tax on that $5,000. Instead, you will end up paying taxes on that money in the long-run.

Obtain a W9 tax form online and have your hired help fill it out. You will need this when you do your own taxes. The 1099 form is the form you will have to fill out at the end of the year. There are different types of 1099 forms, so be sure to read about independent contractors and forms on the IRS website (irs.gov). If you can hire a CPA (certified public accountant) to handle your taxes, I would highly recommend it.

If you do hire someone, make sure that you pay them with a check, and create a ledger of when you pay them and how much. This will come in use when you are doing your taxes. At the end of the year, you will have to figure out exactly how much you paid them for the whole year. If you have a ledger, you can easily add up the total of all checks paid out. If you do not have a ledger, you will have to spend a lot of time going through your bank account to figure this out.

HIRE A VIRTUAL ASSISTANT

Hire a self-employed Virtual Assistant (VA) to help you run your business. A VA is an actual person who works for you as a freelancer. If you become very busy, you may want to hire someone to help with your Etsy messages, marketing efforts, or other day-to-day tasks. VAs are a great way to free up your time so that you can spend it producing more of your quality products.

Look at websites like Upwork, Zirtual, and Fancy Hands. On Upwork, freelancers post their profiles and hourly fees. You can browse people by location and services offered. You can hire a designer, writer, accountant, customer service rep, marketing expert, photographer, or web developer.

Fancy Hands is a network of remote assistants that assist you with a variety of tasks. Their pool of virtual assistants are standing by to help you make a dinner reservation, find you a hairstylist, set a vet appointment or research the best hotel in Austin for you. Want someone to email your mom for you? They can do that. They will do it as long as it's legal and it can be done remotely. The Premier Plan is $199.99 per month and includes 50 requests.

HIRE A CPA

Consider hiring a Certified Public Accountant (CPA) to assist you with your personal and business taxes. A CPA is licensed and current with federal and state tax laws and must participate in continuing education to maintain their license. Unlike an accountant, a CPA can represent you if you are ever audited by the IRS.

You can decide how much assistance you will require. CPAs can assist you with quarterly and annual taxes. CPAs can also be more hands-on, helping you with invoices, accounts payable, payroll, financial statements, and budgets. A CPA can also perform an in-depth financial analysis, providing you a detailed report of your business's health.

You probably won't need full-time tax help in the beginning, but it's nice to know ahead of time what services your CPA offers. Make sure you discuss this with any CPA prior to hiring them. If you are not experienced with accounting and don't want to be personally liable for any accounting mistakes, I recommend hiring a CPA. Typically, the money they will end up saving you is worth the amount you pay them.

MENTORS

Have you ever operated a business? Will your Etsy shop be your first sole proprietorship or partnership? Going into business for yourself doesn't have to be scary or a trial-by-fire. Fortunately, there are volunteers and mentors across the country who can assist you.

SCORE (score.org) is a non-profit organization that is supported by the SBA and has thousands of business mentors around the country that will mentor you. You can visit their website (score.org) and sign up to be paired with a local mentor.

SCORE also offers webinars and online courses. Take an online course in how to create a website, build your brand, or how to write a business plan. They offer dozens of online courses and local workshops that are available on demand. If you're new to operating a business, visit score.org and see how they can help you succeed.

Chapter 7 – Shipping

GET THE BEST DEAL ON SHIPPING

Shipping is a huge part of your Etsy business. Without it, you simply wouldn't make any money. Try to keep your shipping costs as low as possible. If your shop becomes successful, shipping will most likely be your second biggest cost (the first, of course, will be supplies/raw goods).

It's wise to shop around for the best deals on shipping and supplies. There are many companies that sell packaging, labels, tape, etc. Check your local vendors for the best deals. Buying from an unknown local supplier is usually a lot cheaper than buying from a well-known nationwide supplier. I was able to find a local supplier who delivered to my house for just $5 if my order was over $100.

Don't settle for the first shipping company that you feel okay using. There are a couple of huge shipping companies, as you know, but their rates are not all the same. A lot of it depends on where you live. If you are shipping small packages that can easily ship with the U.S. Postal Service, then go that route if you can.

If you are shipping large packages, call UPS and FedEx and ask talk to a local account manager. Set up a time for them to come by and talk to you in person. Explain your business and ask them about discounted rates for frequent shippers. Chances are that they will want to secure your business and will provide a discount.

OFFER FREE SHIPPING

People love finding things that ship for free, and so does the Etsy search engine. Listings that offer free shipping rank higher in the Etsy search algorithm. If you can offer free shipping, do it.

Free shipping doesn't mean that customers aren't paying for shipping. It just means that you factor the cost of shipping into the final price of the product. If you can offer free shipping and not kill your profit, then by all means do it. People will be more willing to buy from your shop if you offer free shipping.

My business was table production, and tables cost a lot to ship. I wasn't able to offer free shipping, but I did offer flat rate shipping for most tables. $59 would ship a large table nationwide. Sometimes I would make a little profit, but usually I took a hit, meaning that my profit margin per table went down due to the steep cost of shipping.

If you're lucky, smart, or both, your products won't cost a lot to ship nationwide. You may even be able to make a little profit that will help cover the cost of shipping, packaging, labels, tape, etc. If you can break even on shipping costs, consider that a win. Don't offer free shipping, however, if it's going to kill your profit and drive your business into the ground. Shoppers prefer free shipping, but they will still pay a reasonable amount if they really want your product.

INTERNATIONAL SHIPPING

Shipping to other countries can be a tedious process, but is it worth the pain? That is up to you to decide. If you want to reach a wider audience, you may want to offer to ship worldwide. Or, you have the option to hand select which countries you will ship to when you create a listing.

When you create a new listing, you will have to set up the shipping information every time, or you can create a shipping profile so that you can use the same setting in future listings. You can create one profile for shipping in the U.S., and you can create another profile for shipping to Canada and Mexico, for example. Having these separate profiles will make it easier for when you create more listings and want to use the same settings.

Offering shipping to other countries and overseas can help boost your sales. If you only offer shipping to the U.S., most international Etsy users will not see your shop or your listings. Shipping overseas, however, will require more time and more paperwork, of course. Be prepared to have to fill out customs forms, and you will definitely want to familiarize yourself with these forms. There may also be associated fees or duties that you and your customer will want to know about.

In my experience with international shipping, the paperwork was the biggest hassle. On top of that, there's the issue of lost or damaged items. I once shipped a pair of tables to Australia, and after traveling thousands of miles, the tables were damaged in transit. The customer did not want a refund, but they did want two new tables. I had to make two additional tables as a result, so I lost money and time on that order. If you ship overseas, you may earn more money in the long-term, but you will possibly have to deal with more issues that will cost you even more time and money.

USE ETSY SHIPPING

You can use Etsy's built-in shipping system, or you may decide to open a separate account with one of the big shipping companies, like FedEx or UPS. If you use Etsy shipping, it will save you time. It is synced with your account so the shipping addresses and information transfer seamlessly. The downside, however, is that Etsy shipping is only set up for USPS shipping. If you are shipping small or medium-sized items in the U.S., Etsy's internal shipping system is probably a wise choice for you.

Another nice thing about Etsy shipping is that they send the customer a shipping notification email. Even if you create and print the label today but set it up to ship two days from now, Etsy will send the customer a shipping notification in two days. You can also include an emailed note to the customer if you want to. It's a great system that they have created for users to help simplify their overall process.

If you are shipping larger items both nationally and internationally, you will probably need to open an account with one of the big shipping companies. I use FedEx to ship my tables, and I've had a good experience using them. Very rarely have I had any issues with lost or damaged items. Call to speak with an account representative, and try to get a deal on bulk shipping if you only use them to ship.

RETURN AND EXCHANGE POLICY

You will have to decide whether you will accept returns or exchanges. This is something that can either help or hinder your sales. Some customers will only buy a product if they know ahead of time that they can return or exchange an item. Some customers don't care what your policy is and will order from you regardless.

I do not accept returns on Etsy, but I do accept exchanges. All of my table items are made-to-order. I do not have an inventory of items ready to ship. Since each item is custom made, I simply cannot afford to do business if people were able to return my items with no questions asked. Because of this, I do not offer returns.

However, I felt that I could afford to offer exchanges because people were less likely to exchange their table for another custom table. The time involved is generally too much for most people to want to deal with it. Additionally, repacking and shipping a table is a major pain. So, I took a gamble and I only offer exchanges in lieu of returns. The gamble has paid off because only 1 in 200 customers want to do an exchange.

You will have to figure out what your policy will be. Can you afford to offer returns? How many people do you think will want to return something? Should you offer exchanges? How many of those can you afford to do? Whatever you decide, make your policy very clear and concise. Also make it clear who pays the return shipping cost.

ORDER CANCELLATIONS

Like your Returns and Exchanges policy, you will need to decide if you accept cancellations. People change their mind, and they also like to know that if they do, they can cancel their order. While this isn't great for you, it is simply just a part of doing business online.

Most people will not cancel their order, so it's a good idea to accept cancellations. If someone needs to cancel, they usually have a legitimate reason to do so. If you handle it professionally and tell them that you hope that they will return and order from you in the future, they will leave your shop feeling better about you and your business practices. You want them to feel that it was not a hassle to cancel their order and that you did not have a problem with it. They might come back in a week or in a month and order from you because you were professional and made a good impression on them.

I accept cancellations within 24 hours of the order being placed. If someone contacts me after the 24 hours is up, I normally still accept the cancellation, given that I have not started to make the item. People will come back to your shop, especially if you treat them well and make sure they know that you appreciate their business.

INVOICING

Don't waste your time creating and printing out an invoice to mail to your customers, as most people don't want an invoice. In all my time selling on Etsy, I have had only one customer ask me for an invoice. That is one person out of over 1,000 customers.

Instead, spend your time and money on a thank you card or include a small gift with every purchase. A thank you card is money well-spent. It tells the customer that you appreciate their business and you hope that they will order from you again.

An invoice tells the customer what they bought from you, but they already know this and can go on Etsy and see what they ordered. If they really need an invoice, they will ask you for one. Invoices are necessary if you are doing B2B sales, but most likely you are not.

Chapter 8 – Etsy-specifics

ETSY SEARCH

Etsy has its own search tool. When someone searches for "yoga mat," for example, the search program looks for keywords (aka tags) that match. The tag words you enter into each of your listings will help people find your items.

Make sure that you complete the tag word section on each new listing you create. You are allowed 13 different tag words per listing. When you create a listing for yoga mats, you should use tag words that are related to yoga and yoga mats: yoga mat, yoga, mat, mats, yogi, exercise, namaste, health, workout, etc.

Etsy also ranks listings based on how well they match the search criteria as well as how well they are performing. A new listing will receive a temporary boost in ranking so that Etsy can monitor its performance and determine how effective it is. Your customer reviews also play a part in your search ranking. If your reviews are mostly five stars and you do not have any open cases against your shop, you will rank even higher.

Believe it or not, the price of your shipping could hurt your ranking. Etsy has found that most people decide to make a purchase based on the cost of shipping. Therefore, if your shipping is viewed as too high, your listings will be ranked lower than others. Listings with free shipping will rank higher. You may want to consider offering free shipping and factor that cost into the overall price.

ETSY POLICIES

Etsy has many policies that you should read before opening your shop. There are policies regarding what you can and cannot sell. There are policies regarding intellectual property rights, anti-discrimination, seller protection, shipping, etc. Read all of them!

- Don't assume that you can open a shop selling something that may not be allowed. There's a list of prohibited items, so don't waste your time creating a shop that may be shut down in a matter of hours or days.

- Etsy allows sellers to partner with approved manufacturers to assist with the making of their product. If you are making items with the help of a third party, you need to make sure that the third party is approved by Etsy first. Visit the Etsy Manufacturing platform to learn more.

- Familiarize yourself with Etsy's fee structure. There are listing fees, transaction fees, payment processing fees, listing renewal fees, in-person selling fees, subscription fees, listing advertising fees, etc. You need to know all of your costs before you can determine your pricing. If you start selling items without knowing the true cost of doing business, you will inevitably be disappointed when you are not making enough profit or maybe even losing money.

ETSY SELLER HANDBOOK

Want to know more about Etsy from the people who run Etsy? Go to the Seller Handbook in the Community and Help section. The Seller Handbook is a compilation of articles and help topics that you can browse or search by topic.

The Seller Handbook covers all topics related to Etsy. Let's say that you want to know more about the Etsy community itself. There are 228 articles available right now. One of those articles is called "Quit Your Day Job: Each To Own." It's an in-depth article about an Australian woman, Kirsten Devitt, who creates laser-cut jewelry. Her Etsy shop Each To Own has over 11,000 sales!

Maybe you want to read more about how to market and brand your shop. There are currently 139 articles that you can learn from. The Seller Handbook is full of free information and ideas. All you have to do is take the time to read them.

ETSY SUBSCRIPTIONS

One important thing that you might overlook on Etsy is the opt-in subscriptions that Etsy offers. It's sort of a hidden gem. To find the Subscriptions page, go to your Account Settings and then click on Emails. Your Subscriptions will show up. You have to click on each one in order to receive them. Make sure you also click Save at the bottom.

This is where you can pick and choose what information Etsy sends to you. You can find information on new trends, how to participate in Etsy research, and even receive updates about your own shop. All of these options exist specifically to help you succeed and to provide you with valuable information.

ETSY TEAMS

Etsy teams are a great way to meet other Etsy sellers so you can learn new strategies. There are some Etsy teams that are more interested in spamming its members or exchanging favorites for the sake of self-promotion. Try to avoid teams that appear to be only about promotion and favoriting if you can.

You can find teams by going to community.etsy.com. You will have to apply to join a team. The approval process will take anywhere from hours to a few days depending on the team. I would apply to just one or two to start, and see how you like them before applying to more.

One way to find a team that is legitimate is to look at the shop owners you like and see if they are members of any teams. From there, write them a message and ask them if they would recommend the team or not. A team referral is a good way to go. "Hi, I love your shop and I see that you are a member of the team _____. I am interested in joining but wanted to know if you would recommend them or not?"

ETSY FORUMS

Etsy Forums is where new and experienced shop owners gather to share learned knowledge. Here you can browse discussion topics or post questions that you may have. Forums can be found in the same place as Etsy Teams, community.etsy.com.

If you are new to Etsy and want to get involved in the community, check out Forums. There are several Forum categories: Announcements, Creative Process, Branding, and Pricing and Finance to name just a few. You can browse Popular Discussions to see what people are talking about today.

If you are new to Etsy and have some questions, get involved with the Etsy community. It's not just an online marketplace; it's a community of entrepreneurs that support one another, care about each other succeeding, and are open to giving advice and sharing information.

ETSY MESSAGES

Etsy has its own messaging system called Conversations. It's very similar to email where you have your Inbox, Sent, Unread, and Trash folders. Customers and potential customers will contact you via this communication system. Like email, messages will come in day and night. You can set up the Etsy app on your phone so that you will receive notifications and can send and receive messages on-the-go.

When I first started out on Etsy, I tried to answer every message in real time. I learned that it's okay to not answer every message right away. People don't expect an instantaneous reply, and it's grueling trying to keep up. Even now, I receive about 10 to 12 messages every day, and I do my best to respond the same day.

The key is to always be professional in your conversations. These are existing or potential customers. Use courteous and professional language every time. Even if you are dealing with someone who's upset or using foul language, do not use the same language back. You may want to respond curtly, but this is your business, and you need to be professional and courteous in your correspondence.

Chapter 9 – Running Your Business

SHOP NAME

The name you choose for your shop is important. It's a business just like any other business. Your shop name should convey your overall product theme and reflect your personal style. Your digital shop could, one day, become a physical business with an actual shop. This is a reason to think long-term when deciding on a name.

First, decide what you will be selling, as this is a big part of the naming strategy. If you are selling handmade yoga mats, you already know that you are leaning toward a healthy lifestyle theme. The theme of your shop should help to determine the name you select.

Next, brainstorm what you might be selling in the future. This is an unknown part of the equation for right now, but it's important to consider. If you plan to create a shop name that only incorporates the yoga mat theme, you might find it difficult to sell handmade sandals a year from now. It's possible that sandals will be your bigger seller, not the yoga mats. "Bob's Yoga Mats" may not be relevant in a year, which would force you to rebrand.

Third, what's the general image that you want to paint inside a potential customer's head with your brand's name? Do you want potential customers to view your business as a yoga mat shop, or do you want them to view it as a healthy lifestyle shop that sells yoga mats and related items?

Finally, think twice before using a geographic location in your name. As an online business, your customers live everywhere. They reside in California, New York, Florida, Alaska, and everywhere in between. Does a shop name with the word "Texas" or "Beach" or "Desert" appeal to a broad audience? If you name your shop "North Dakota Clothing," does the name appeal to everyone? You actually may not be trying to appeal to everyone, but the more appealing your name is to a broad audience, the better.

KEEP IT SIMPLE

You have probably heard of the K.I.S.S. acronym, "keep it simple, stupid." It was used by the U.S. Navy as far back as 1960. It states that most systems work best if they are kept simple and that simplicity should be the goal of design. This is true in both design and business.

You can utilize the "keep it simple" rule when creating your Etsy shop, as you don't have to make it more complicated than it needs to be. Your photography, your listing descriptions, your pricing, your products – all of these can be created so that your customers find it to be clear, concise, and easy to understand.

Make your listings easy to read and easy to understand. Use plain language, and make the descriptions clear and to-the-point. You don't need to write an essay describing each product in detail or where the idea came from. Explain the details, but don't overwhelm the customer with unnecessary information.

Make your pricing simple. Don't complicate things by having ten different price points on one listing because you offer ten different upgrade options. Simple is better. If you must have ten different options for one product, consider having different listings for those upgrades or consider reducing the number of options. You don't want to overwhelm the customer by loading one listing with too many options.

Keep your product offerings as simple as possible. Don't try to tackle every idea that you have in the beginning. If you have 25 different product ideas that you want to offer, maybe start with 12 and see how it goes. You can always add more products later.

Keep your production process simple. It's easy to create one prototype and offer it for sale, but how difficult will it be for you to make 500 or 1,000 copies of that prototype? When you design something that you plan to sell, you need to ask yourself how simple will it be to create it over and over again. Can you alter the design to make the production process faster?

WEEKLY CHECKLIST

Every Monday, I make a list of things that I have to do for that week. I then arrange those tasks by the day. This process keeps me organized, and it keeps me on schedule for production and shipping. Without my checklist, I would definitely forget to do something.

You can either write your checklist on paper or use an app on your phone or computer. Prioritize your checklist by numbering the tasks or use different colors or highlight the "must do" tasks.

It's helpful to designate days to certain tasks. Mondays might be the day that you run errands and buy supplies. Tuesdays and Wednesdays are the days you make new product. Thursdays are when you package, print labels, and send customers the shipping information. Fridays are when you ship and start making more product.

In addition to the "must do" tasks, like production, running errands, emailing customers, and shipping, be sure to leave space so that you can add more tasks as necessary. Having a few blank to-dos every day will allow you to fill those in as the week unfolds. You might get a rush order or need to take the dog to the vet.

TIME MANAGEMENT

Time management is devoting the right amount of time to the right task. If you expect your Etsy shop to be a success, you need to have good time management skills.

You should have a daily routine when it comes to managing your business. Staying motivated and productive when you are self-employed and working at home can be difficult. There will be days where you don't feel like working, even though you know you need to. Make your to-do list and stick to it. If you have a physical list of tasks that need to be completed, you will be more motivated and inclined to accomplish those tasks.

Prioritize the tasks that lie ahead. You might want to spend your time making products, but before you do that you need to have a business plan and you need to do your Etsy research. Making products can wait. Don't spend your time doing something now that you shouldn't be doing yet.

Stay focused. If you know that you must do A and B today in order to accomplish C tomorrow, stick to the plan. Don't do C today and put off A and B until tomorrow. Don't get sidetracked.

Being efficient can be as simple as doing the things that you know you're good at. If you are new at making websites, and you know it's going to take you days or weeks to figure it out, then find someone who can help you create a website. That's time and money well spent.

Wake up an hour earlier. If you find that you don't have enough time in the day to do the things you have to do, simply make more time.

That extra hour in the morning can make a big difference. If you aren't a morning person, then set aside an extra hour at night.

WORK HARDER THAN YOUR COMPETITOR

Simply wanting a successful shop isn't enough -- you have to be willing to put in the hard work, as running your own business isn't an easy task. If you don't have the time and energy to devote to creating and running your Etsy shop, it will not succeed. Your input will directly affect the output.

If you want it bad enough and put in the hard work, you can succeed on Etsy. It's a mistake to think that it will be easy or that Etsy will make it easy for you. Etsy won't run your shop or create your listings, nor will the site respond to potential customers. Etsy provides you with the necessary format and the tools to succeed, but your success is not guaranteed.

Putting in the work and making your Etsy shop the best that it can be will translate to making a profit. One of your goals should be to create the best possible shop that you can. You should also strive to create products that customers will love. If you strive to be the best within your competitive market, there's a good chance that devotion will pay off. Even if your shop isn't actually "the best," you should always strive for the best -- otherwise, what's the point?

I spent hours every day on Etsy before I officially opened my shop. I researched the competition, their products, and their pricing structures. I spent time and energy teaching myself how Etsy worked, looking at the shops that I liked, and planning what I could do to stand out from the crowd. If you don't do this kind of research and don't have a firm understanding of what you need to do, then don't expect much in return.

WORK SMARTER

We have all heard the phrase "work smarter, not harder." If you can implement "working smarter" when running your Etsy business, you will be happy that you did. Working smarter can refer to a number of things:

- Manage your time more effectively – Are you wasting time doing something the wrong way or doing something in the wrong order?
- Do the research – Have you done enough research? Is there something important that you missed?
- Increase your profit margin – Have you exhausted all potential vendors/suppliers/discounts? Is there any way that you can save more money?
- Automate where you can – Can any of your production be automated in an affordable manner? Should you look into Etsy production partners?
- Increase productivity – Can you be more productive by yourself or are you maxed out? Should you hire part-time help to assist you and free up your time?
- Do what you know – Do you have any experience in what you are doing? If so, there's a greater chance that you will succeed. If you are doing something that's unfamiliar to you, consider finding a mentor.
- Know your weaknesses – If you know that you are not good at doing something, like taxes, then do not spend your time doing it alone. Knowing your weaknesses is not being weak -- it's being smart.

THIRD PERSON

Try to view your shop as a customer. It's easy to exist inside your owner and operator bubble and become comfortable. It's also easy to think that everything is going smoothly and that it will continue like that for another year. That may not be true.

It's imperative to step outside your bubble and take a good look at your business as a whole approximately every three months. If you have difficulty stepping back, ask a trusted friend to examine your shop, your listings, your products, and website. Don't be afraid to ask for other people's opinions. You might not like what they tell you, but you need to be open to constructive criticism.

Take the time to stop and examine your shop to make sure that everything looks the way it should and is working properly. Ask yourself:

- Is it time to remove products that aren't selling?
- Is it time to offer new products?
- Should you change your banner image?
- Do you need to update your policies or edit your story?
- Does your website need to be updated?
- Are the links still working properly?

BE A MANAGER

Do you have management experience? If so, you probably have the necessary skills to run and manage a small business. You don't need to have management experience, of course, but it does help to have the managerial skillset.

Managers are typically good at problem solving, delegating, organization, multi-tasking, and customer service. Problem solving is a huge part of running your own business. Issues will inevitably arise, and you will have to decide, usually by yourself, what action to take to solve the problem. If you have difficulty solving problems, there won't be anyone there to make the right decision for you.

Delegating is another big part of running a small business. You will need to decide which tasks you should perform by yourself and in which order to perform them, and then you will need to decide which tasks should be performed by your business partner (if you have one) or by a freelancer or employee (if you hire one).

Being organized and being able to multi-task are valuable qualities when operating a small business. If these are not your strengths, you will likely need help running your business.

THE CUSTOMER IS YOUR BOSS

Like it or not, the customer is essentially your boss. Your boss at any regular job is the person who gives you money, reviews your work, has expectations of you, and believes in your ability to do whatever it is that you do. How are your customers any different?

Seeing each customer as your boss will help keep you accountable. When you're self-employed and work from home, sometimes it can be difficult to self-motivate. You don't have a boss looking over your shoulder, so it's easy to drag your feet and put things off. You are in charge now, and you decide how things get done.

What if you get a message from a customer, and they want to know where their order is? Why is their order one day late? What is happening? At that point, you'll feel motivated. You'll realize that you do indeed have someone to answer to: your customers.

CUSTOMER IDEAS

Most customers won't contact you on Etsy; they'll simply place their order, and that will be it. A small percentage of customers will offer you unsolicited ideas, and some of those ideas are worth implementing.

Listen to them. If more than one customer gives you similar feedback that you perceive as negative, like, "I can't figure out the options in your listing," you should immediately review the way that your listing is written. It's possible that the wording is clear to you, but if others are having difficulty understanding it, you need to rework it. Don't take all constructive criticism as negative. Try to extract the constructive aspect. Some people are truly trying to help you make your business better.

Some customers will have good ideas for your shop or introduce a product that you may have overlooked. They might suggest a color, style, or design that you had never considered. They could give you ideas that you can use to make your business better and increase your revenue.

CUSTOMER REVIEWS

You want people to have a great buying experience so that they will not only buy from you again, but so that they will tell their friends and family about your shop. You also want people to write a positive review and to give you five stars. Reviews will be read by potential customers, who will then decide whether or not they want to trust you with their business.

Most people read the reviews, especially if they are new to your shop and want to see what others are saying about your business. If your products and pricing are terrific but you have terrible reviews, there's a good chance that people will spend their money elsewhere. If your products and pricing are average, but your reviews are terrific, there's a good chance that people will buy from you. In short, reviews are important, especially in today's digital world and many platforms of communication.

How do you get five-star reviews? First, provide five-star customer service. Answer people's messages in a timely manner. Be kind. Be empathetic to any issues that may arise. Use professional and friendly language all the time. Offer to refund part or all their money if there is an issue. Ship on time.

How do you get *bad* reviews? Ignore the customer. Don't respond to messages in a timely manner. Don't be professional in your language. Refuse to compensate the customer when an issue arises. Don't ship product when you say you will.

What can you do about a bad review? If you receive a horrible review, I would recommend contacting the customer immediately. Be courteous and professional in your message, even if their review was mean or you feel that it was inaccurate. Apologize to the customer, be sympathetic, and ask what you can do to make it right. An apology goes a long way with most people.

UNDER PROMISE AND OVER DELIVER

One way to get great reviews and to have happy customers is to do what you say you will do. It's that simple. Another way is to under promise and over deliver.

Let's look at shipping, for example. If you tell everyone that you ship in three to four weeks, but you actually ship in two to three weeks, you are delivering the product to the customer a week earlier than expected. Most customers will be excited to receive their items a week early and most will be very happy about this.

Of course, there are exceptions to this. The customer could be out of town when you ship. One way to avoid any shipping issues is to send the customer a shipping notification one day prior to actually shipping the product. The customer will receive the notification and can contact you if there is a potential issue about delivery confirmation.

Another good way to under promise and over deliver is to include the free gift with every purchase. Whether or not the customer actually uses the gift is not important. It's the thought that counts. You could also send the customer a $10 Etsy gift card, for example, and a message thanking them for their business. Because of that one simple move, there's a great chance that they will spend the $10 gift card at your shop.

CREATE A BRAND

A brand is more than a logo. A brand is everything that encapsulates your business: the logo, look, product, perception, and emotion. When you think about a brand name like Coca-Cola, you don't just picture the logo: you know the product, the taste, the colors, the ads, and you most likely have an emotional connection.

A logo is an important aspect of a brand. Nike. Apple. Ford. McDonald's. You can see those logos in your mind. We know them very well. A logo is what sets different brands apart, but a brand isn't the logo by itself.

A brand exists mostly inside the mind of the consumer. You try to craft a brand image for the customer, but people will have different impressions of your brand. Your description of Coca-Cola, for example, would be heavily influenced by your personal experiences, preferences and tastes.

What brand image will you create? What do you want your customer to feel when they think about your brand? Are you even trying to create a brand? These are things to consider when you are starting your business. Your Etsy shop can become a brand of itself.

FREQUENTLY ASKED QUESTIONS

You will find that people will ask you a lot of the same questions. One way to avoid receiving so many messages is to create an identical FAQ section on both your Etsy page and your website. You'll find that having this available for your customers will save you a tremendous amount of time.

Create your FAQ with a few popular questions to begin with:

- How long does production take?
- How much is shipping?
- Do you do custom work?
- Do you ship internationally?
- Do you offer refunds or exchanges?
- Do you offer rush/expedited service?

To come up with your FAQs, look at your shop the way a potential customer would. What are the most likely questions someone might ask you? Even though you create a FAQ, people will still message you and ask questions, of course, but the FAQ will ultimately save you time by not having to answer so many messages.

YOUR STORY

When I visit a shop, one of the first things I do is click on the shop owner. I like to read their story, the About section. Many times, there is no information. I'm surprised that so many shop owners choose to not share their story. Maybe they don't want to tell people or maybe they don't feel that they have a story to tell. Everyone has a story.

You should share your story on Etsy. Etsy is a marketplace and a community of artisans. Many Etsy customers like to know who the person is behind the shop. You are interesting! You may not think so, but other people may want to get to know you and your story.

You don't have to write a long bio. You can write a paragraph or two. Your story can help connect you with potential customers. People that find you relatable are more likely to follow you, to like your shop, and to order from you. More relatable = more sales.

Why do you do what you do? How long have you been doing it? What are some of your favorite things? What brought you to Etsy? We can all answer these questions. Now, all you have to do is turn that into a paragraph or two.

INTELLECTUAL PROPERTY

You may be a good person with only good intentions, but there are some devious people in the world. Etsy is no exception. There will be some people on Etsy who are, let's say, opportunists. They will do whatever they want to help their shop succeed, including stealing someone's intellectual property.

Intellectual property (IP) includes creations of the human intellect, such as copyrights, trademarks, and patents. It also includes artistic designs, inventions, symbols, music, and literature. People who knowingly copy something are committing what is called infringement, whether it be copyright, trademark, or patent. Infringement is reproducing, distributing, or making derivative works without permission.

Simply put, do not copy or steal people's work. Someone will eventually notice and will report you. Etsy is a community of artisans and business people who generally look out for each other.

COPYRIGHTS AND TRADEMARKS

Are you creating products that have your original designs or artwork that you want to protect? Do you want to trademark your unique business name? Is your logo a design that needs to be trademarked? These are all things to consider if you do not want other people to copy your original work.

If you want to protect your product photos, you can place a watermark on your listing photos. A watermark won't give you legal protection, but it can deter theft and reuse. If you have a program like Photoshop, you can easily place a watermark on your photos.

If you are creating original artwork and want to protect it, you may want to consider copyright protection. You can copyright original paintings, drawings, digital art, photographs, literary works, movies, and more. Go to copyright.gov to learn more about copyrights and what you can do to protect your work.

If you want to register a trademark, you will need to conduct a search at uspto.gov. If you are creating a brand name and want to protect it nationwide, it is a good idea to register it on the federal level. You can also choose to file for a state trademark. Because of the intricate nature of trademark registration, I would recommend hiring an attorney to assist you with this process.

Don't forget to register your business name (aka trade name) with your county or state. A trade name is your DBA or "doing business as" name. Check with your local SBA (Small Business Administration) office to find out how to register your trade name.

OBTAIN AN E.I.N.

If you form a partnership, corporation or non-profit, you will need to obtain an Employer Identification Number (EIN). An EIN is a Federal Tax ID Number assigned to your business by the IRS. If you are an individual/sole proprietor, you are not required to have an EIN.

Sole proprietors use their Social Security Number to file business tax returns. Other businesses, such as partnerships, use their EIN to file taxes. An EIN is similar to a SSN in that the IRS uses it to identify the taxpayer. However, the EIN is not considered sensitive information, like a SSN.

If you are a sole proprietor and would rather have an EIN, you can obtain one. For my Etsy business, I have an EIN because my business became a S Corp. I also pay a CPA to handle everything, and it is worth every penny. If you have questions about EINs and what is right for your business, I would recommend speaking with a CPA.

BUSINESS LIFE SPAN

Every business has a beginning, middle, and an end. An Etsy business is just like any other business, so expect it to peak or plateau at some point. Hopefully, that's a long time from now.

The average lifespan for any business, big or small, ranges from eight to 10 years. Understanding the realistic trajectory of your business is a wise and practical approach to managing the day-to-day operations. Doing this will keep you grounded in reality and will help you make smart financial decisions.

Let's say that your Etsy shop averages $4,000 per month for a few consecutive months. When this happens, it's easy to expect that to be the new norm. You may start thinking that it will continue in this pattern, like a steady paycheck. But, in reality, you cannot expect anything to remain constant.

If you spend wisely, there's a good chance that your business will last longer. For example, if your sales of 3D printed dog figurines are slowing down, but you really want to purchase that new, expensive 3D printer, you'll conclude that maybe now is not the right time. You can instead find a used printer that's perhaps half the price.

FAILURE IS OKAY

It's okay to fail. You will learn from your mistakes. As long as you do learn and make changes, the failure was meaningful. You can try again.

Your first Etsy shop might not work out the way you had planned. Perhaps it brought in some income, but maybe it wasn't a big hit. That's okay. You can revamp it, shut it down, or create another shop if you want to. If it isn't working for you, sometimes the best thing to do is to cut your losses and move on.

Knowing when to close shop is difficult, but it's necessary to be able to identify when a business is not working. You invest a lot of time, energy, and money into starting a business -- you don't want to spend more time and more money trying to keep a sinking ship afloat.

Of course, you don't want your business to fail. Take it as a learning experience and move on. Failing is just part of learning and growing. Afterall: F.A.I.L. = First Attempt In Learning.

WORK-LIFE BALANCE

Having a healthy work-life balance is crucial to your wellbeing. When my Etsy shop became successful, I had to do everything myself. I was working at home, which is great, but I was working six or seven days per week.

At some point, working too much will catch up to you. You can do everything yourself until you just can't. If your shop does well and you find yourself working all of the time, it's a good idea to take time to review your operation.

First, ask yourself what you are doing that someone else could help with. For me, I was spending at least eight hours per week sanding wood. I enjoy sanding, but if I could have someone do that for me, it would free up eight hours of my time every week. So, I hired a part-time sander.

Set normal working hours. In the beginning, I answered every Etsy message from a customer or potential customer as fast as possible, no matter the hour of the day. I was determined to respond to messages quickly because I didn't want to lose out on a potential sale. Now, if a message comes in after 8pm, my response waits until the morning. Even though you work from home, you should still set normal working hours for yourself.

If you are seriously busy, it will be difficult for you to not work. The problem is that even if you work seven days a week, you will still have orders to fulfill. It's a good problem to have, but you need to set time aside time to relax and unplug. No matter what – no matter how much pressure you're under – take at least one day off from work every week. You deserve time off.

ADDITIONAL SALES CHANNELS

Etsy is terrific, but if this becomes your full-time business and your primary source of income, you need to think about your financial future. In addition to Etsy, there are other ways that you can sell your products: your website, Amazon, Ebay, etc. It's a good idea to explore additional sales channels in today's digital world of consumption.

Having a website independent of Etsy is a great start. Etsy offers an integrated website builder called Pattern, but it is not an independent entity like GoDaddy or Weebly. If Etsy were to shut down, your Pattern website would likely become useless. Consider selling your products on a website that is not connected to Etsy. That way, if anything were to happen with the Etsy platform, you can still take orders online and promote your website.

If your Etsy shop is a success, look at selling your products on Amazon and Ebay, too. You can sell on Amazon as an individual or professional. Individuals can sell up to 40 items per month, and professionals can sell 40+ items per month. There are different monthly fees and selling fees depending on your plan. The professional plan has more features, but it also costs more.

Whatever you do, it's important to explore additional sales channels, especially if Etsy becomes your only source of income. You don't want to rely solely on one marketplace forever because things could change in the future, and you need to be prepared. Etsy will likely be around for a long time, but you just never know. Remember to not put all your eggs in one basket.

DON'T GIVE UP

It's hard to be patient sometimes. You have created this incredible shop with a lot of listings, and you're wondering where all the customers are. I've been there. You just have to be patient and make sure that you're doing all that you can to get the word out. If you're doing everything right, it's only a matter of time before you start getting customers.

Here's a checklist for marketing your shop:

1. Promote your shop on social media
2. Tell your friends via email, text, and social media
3. Set up Promoted Listings on Etsy
4. Link to your Etsy shop on social media
5. Link listings to other listings on Etsy
6. Create a website
7. Link your website to Etsy and link Etsy to your website
8. Set up a Google Ads account
9. Set up a Pinterest ad account
10. Set up a Facebook and Instagram ad account
11. Take amazing photos and post them everywhere
12. Set up Etsy's Abandoned Cart and Recently Favorited promotions
13. Have a sale
14. Go to community.etsy.com and create an announcement
15. Create new listings
16. Use different tag words in your listings
17. Distribute a press release to media and blogs
18. Hire a social media marketing company
19. Offer free shipping
20. Keep promoting!

The information in this book should not be construed as legal or professional tax advice. Consult an attorney or tax professional to determine what is best for you and your business.

Printed in Great Britain
by Amazon